THE MUSEUM OF THE CITY OF NEW YORK

Portraits of America

Ellis Island

THE MUSEUM OF THE CITY OF NEW YORK

Portraits of America

Ellis Island

John S. Berman

BARNES
&NOBLE
BOOKS
NEW YORK

A BARNES & NOBLE BOOK

©2003 by Barnes & Noble Publishing, Inc.

Library of Congress Cataloging-in-Publication Data

Berman, John S.
      Ellis Island / John S. Berman.
            p. cm. — (Portraits of America)
      At head of title: The Museum of the City of New York.
      Includes bibliographical references and index.
      ISBN 0-7607-3888-2 (alk. paper)
         1. Ellis Island Immigration Station (N.Y. and N.J.)—History. Museum of
      the City of
New York. II.Title. III. Series.

      JV6484 .B47 2003
      304.8'73—dc21

                                                                2002038477

Editor: Betsy Beier
Art Director: Kevin Ullrich
Designer: Liz Trovato
Photography Editor: Lori Epstein
Digital Imaging: Daniel J. Rutkowski
Production Manager: Richela Fabian Morgan

Color separations by Bright Arts Graphics (S) Pte Ltd.
Printed and bound in China by C&C Offset Printing Co. Ltd.

10 9 8 7 6 5 4 3 2 1

About the Museum of the City of New York

The Museum of the City of New York is one of New York City's great cultural treasures—the first U.S. museum dedicated to the study of a single city. Founded in 1923, it presents the nearly four hundred–year evolution of one of history's most important metropolises through exhibitions, educational programs, and publications, and by collecting and preserving the artifacts that tell New York's remarkable stories.

The Museum's collection of 1.5 million objects reflects the diverse and dramatic history of New York City. In addition to prints and photographs, the Museum collects and preserves paintings and sculptures, costumes, theater memorabilia, decorative arts and furniture, police and fire fighting materials, toys made or used in New York, material related to the history of the port, and thousands of varied objects and documents that illuminate the lives of New Yorkers, past and present. Among the gems of the collections are gowns worn at George Washington's inaugural ball, New York's last surviving omnibus and one of its last Checker Cabs, archives of the work of renowned photographers Jacob A. Riis and Berenice Abbott, the world's largest collection of Currier & Ives prints, and pieces of the Times Square news "zipper."

Through its Department of Learning, the Museum offers programs to thousands of teachers and students from all five boroughs every year, including guided tours, teacher training, and its annual New York City History Day contest—the nation's largest urban history fair. Other activities for audiences of all ages include hands-on workshops, performances, book readings, scholarly conferences and lectures, films, and walking tours.

The Museum's rich collections and archives are available to the public for research. To learn how to explore the collections or how to order reproductions of images, visit the Museum's website at www.mcny.org. The website also features exhibition previews, up-to-date program information, an on-line Museum shop, virtual exhibitions, student aids, and information on how you can support the Museum's work.

MUSEUM OF THE
CITY OF NEW YORK
1220 Fifth Avenue
New York, NY 10029
(212) 534-1672
www.mcny.org

Contents

Above: A throng of new arrivals waits under the cast-iron-and-glass canopy outside the imposing edifice of the main building.

Ellis Island and Its Legacy

The name "Ellis Island" evokes myriad historical associations—both positive and negative—with the great wave of immigration from southern and eastern Europe that took place in America in the late nineteenth and early twentieth centuries. Referred to by would-be immigrants as both the "Island of Hope" and the "Island of Tears"— the latter an indication of the often harsh conditions and disappointments suffered there—Ellis Island was the port of entry for as many as five thousand to ten thousand people per day during its busiest period, from 1900 to 1914. From 1892, when the island officially opened as a federal immigration station, to its abandonment in 1954, twelve million of the sixteen million new arrivals to the United States entered through Ellis Island. In 1907 alone, more than one million people passed through its doors. It is estimated that as many as 40 percent of all current U.S. citizens can trace some part of their ancestry to Ellis Island, making this tiny island in the upper New York Bay near the New Jersey coast the most important immigrant processing center in American history.

Ellis Island also served as a mirror of sorts to America's ambivalent attitude toward immigration as the country shifted from a primarily agrarian society to a more industrial one, with cities taking on a newfound importance. The immigration station opened at a time when the flow of people from northern and western Europe had begun to slow and newcomers from eastern and southern Europe were arriving en masse. Even during the peak immigration years before World War I, when the United States had a relatively liberal immigration policy, there remained a deep divide among political leaders as to which "aliens" were desirable for entry into the country, with many politicians viewing the new arrivals in an unabashedly negative light.

When Ellis Island and other federal immigrant stations were opened on the East and West Coasts, the Chinese Exclusion Act had been in effect for ten years. Other proposals to limit the flow of immigrants were hotly debated in Congress in the last two decades of the nineteenth century. Laws were eventually passed that denied entry not only to people with physical and mental illnesses, but also to so-called "undesirables," including polygamists, prostitutes, and contract laborers (i.e., immigrants imported to work for a particular company). Certain politicians never stopped pushing for immigration restrictions and for the deportation of suspected enemy aliens. Their arguments began to hold sway after World War I.

The federal government's decision to create the immigration station on Ellis Island reflected two distinct political pulls: one to reform immigration by taking it away from New York State, which had been accused of mismanagement and the mistreatment of newcomers at its immigration station; the other to regulate immigration by creating a more systematic method of processing new arrivals and determining who would be allowed into the United States. From its inception, Ellis Island was meant to be used primarily as an inspection center for poor immigrants, those who rode "steerage," in the lowest levels of the ships. Immigrants who had the money for a first- or second-class ticket were generally processed onboard and allowed to pass directly into New York City or New Jersey.

By the turn of the century, despite the long, grueling voyage, the difficult and sometimes humiliating inspections, and the new rules on the books attempting to prevent the entry of anyone who might become a "public charge," thousands of immigrants flowed through Ellis Island. Increasingly, these newcomers arrived from eastern and southern Europe rather than from the northern and western countries, which had furnished most of the previous generation of immigrants. Although thousands were turned away at Ellis Island, the vast majority successfully entered the United States and many became citizens, in no small measure because of the tremendous need for labor in the fast-growing economy.

Jews fleeing the pogroms in Czarist Russia and Italians escaping their impoverished homeland are perhaps the best known of the new immigrant groups that arrived at the turn of the century, but there were also Poles, Hungarians, Serbs, Czechs, Slovaks, and Greeks, forced to

Below: In a political cartoon illustrating the contentious nature of the immigration debate in the last two decades of the nineteenth century, President Benjamin Harrison recommends the restriction of newcomers as he is hounded by foreign representatives wanting to enter America.

PRESIDENT HARRISON RECOMMENDS RESTRICTION OF IMMIGRATION.

leave their homes because of war, drought, famine, or religious persecution. Migrants from non-European countries such as Syria, Turkey, and Armenia also passed through Ellis Island on what they hoped would be the final stop on their long voyage to the New World.

Because images of Ellis Island during this period are so prevalent, and the history they document so resonant in the popular imagination, it is easy for the mystique of the site to overwhelm its reality, and for the immigrants passing through the gates of the processing station to be romanticized into the "huddled masses" of American folklore. The reality of Ellis Island is best understood as a collection of many individual voices. Each one of the millions of immigrants who left his or her native country and undertook the long and difficult journey to America brought a unique story upon arriving at the immigration station in New York. Their lives and experiences make up the history of Ellis Island.

Above: The main building on Ellis Island, seen here from Island Two, was considered an architectural gem even in its day.

Left: Immigrant families frequently came to America dressed in the traditional clothing of their homelands. These people may have come from the Balkans.

Above: A Swedish woman hands her ticket to officials as she boards the ferry that will take her from the New York dock, where her ship landed, to Ellis Island.

Above: An Italian woman and her child wait outside a caged detention cell.

Above: The new immigration station during the last stages of construction in June 1900. The reconstruction project took more than three years to complete at a cost of $1.5 million.

CHAPTER ONE

The Early Years

In the seventeenth century, Ellis Island was known as Kioshk, or Gull Island, by the Mohegan tribe that populated parts of Manhattan. It was so named because only seagulls seemed to be able to live on the island's scant two or three acres (0.8–1.2ha) of mud and clay, barely discernible above high tide in upper New York Bay.

After purchasing the island in 1630, the colonial government of New Amsterdam began calling it Oyster Island because of the discovery of the succulent shellfish on its beaches. Manhattan's early settlers, however, didn't view the island as being particularly valuable, and it changed ownership several times. During the 1700s, it took on the inauspicious name of Gibbet Island, as it was then the site of the grisly execution by hanging of a number of convicted criminals, most notably a pirate known as "Anderson," using a gibbet, or gallows tree.

The name Ellis Island came from Samuel Ellis, who purchased the property around the time of the Revolutionary War. Ellis made a number of unsuccessful attempts to sell the island, including a notice he posted in the January 20, 1785, edition of *Loudon's New York Packet* offering a "pleasant situated Island, called Oyster Island, lying in York Bay . . . together with all its improvements, which are considerable." Upon Ellis's death in 1794, the members of his family entered a long and nasty dispute over the title to the land. In 1808, the state purchased the land for what a committee of New Yorkers had deemed to be its fair value of "no less than $10,000." It was immediately ceded to the federal government (with due compensation to the state of New York), for the building of Fort Gibson, completed just prior to the outbreak of the War of 1812. As it turned out, however, the U.S. Army had little need for Fort Gibson except as a place to store ammunition, and it was dismantled by the government in 1861. The navy used Ellis Island as a munitions depot for a number of years until 1890, when the House Committee on Immigration selected it to be the new site of the immigration station for the Port of New York. This new station replaced Castle Garden, at the Battery in lower Manhattan, which had been closed after congressional investigations found evidence of system-wide corruption, political cronyism, and mismanagement.

Castle Garden, opened in 1855 as the nation's first immigrant receiving station, saw eight million new arrivals pass through its doors over its thirty-five-year history. New York authorities had viewed Castle Garden—once a popular concert hall, but since fallen into decline—as an ideal location for the processing of immigrants, who had previously been allowed to enter directly into the city after passing through customs.

Above: Ellis Island's new federal immigration station under construction in 1899. The original station was built of pine, and burned to the ground in 1897—just five years after it opened. After the event, Immigration Commissioner Joseph Senner commented to the *New York Tribune* that "a row of unsightly, ramshackle tinderboxes has been removed, and when the government rebuilds, it will be forced to put up decent fireproof structures."

The Castle Garden immigration depot had been developed, in part, to determine which immigrants were acceptable for entry into the country. Nonwhite, non-European newcomers, who were in the minority, were likely to be detained and eventually sent home, but those permitted to enter hardly had an easy transition to life in America. Thieves and con men lurked around the wharves of Castle Garden, preying on naive and frightened immigrants. By the 1880s, several New York City newspapers were reporting widespread mistreatment and abuse by immigration officials themselves. Joseph Pulitzer's newspaper *The World* also cited cases of immigrants being detained "for no good reason" and given only bread and milk to eat. In one case, according to *The World*, a Norwegian immigrant was criminally attacked by one of the employees at Castle Garden. U.S. Treasury Secretary William Windom declared in 1890 that if Washington was to succeed in ferreting out the corruption that had developed in immigration, it must further isolate the newcomers upon arrival. Although Windom's first choice was Bedloe (now Liberty) Island, the site of the newly built Statue of Liberty, Congress opted to locate the station on Ellis Island, in part because it gave the federal government a rationale for removing the naval munitions, which had been a source of protest by residents of New York and New Jersey.

The tiny, muddy island, however, was hardly equipped to take on this major new role. In order to adequately serve as an immigrant processing station, Ellis Island had to be enlarged by 3.3 acres (1.3ha) through landfill brought in from the excavation of subway tunnels and Grand Central Station. Building engineers constructed a ferry slip and new docks, and a channel was dredged to a depth of more than twelve feet (3.7m). The need for fresh water meant that wells and cisterns also had to be dug.

Over the course of the next two years, Ellis Island expanded to fourteen acres (5.6ha), and its main immigration station—a two-story, 400-foot-long (122m), 150-foot-wide (46m) building constructed of Georgia pine, with a slate roof—was completed. *Harper's Weekly* called the new edifice "a latter-day watering place hotel presenting to the view a great many-windowed expanse of buff-painted wooden walls." The main building included baggage rooms on the ground level and an impressive, albeit imposing, inspection hall on the second floor, with a fifty-six-foot (17m) vaulted ceiling. Smaller structures followed in short order, including a detainee dormitory, a restaurant, a kitchen, a baggage station, and a small hospital. The price tag on the immigration station at the time of its opening on January 1, 1892, had reached a staggering half a million dollars. But that was just the beginning. All during the 1890s, work on Ellis Island continued, even as immigrants made their way through the station. Despite the impressive architectural achievement, the new employees hired to work in the Registry Room constantly complained of leaky roofs and expressed fear that the building would collapse in the winter. Several architects reported structural defects in the design and the use of substandard materials in construction.

Work on the station had finally approached official completion in June 1897 when a massive fire erupted in the kitchen of the main building. In the span of only an hour, the slate roof of the main building collapsed and every one of the pine buildings burned to the ground. The former ammunition vaults, which held all the old immigration records going back to Castle Garden, were also completely destroyed. Amazingly, no one was killed or injured during the fire; only two hundred immigrants were on the island at the time.

Over the next three years, the immigration station was closed and newcomers, who began arriving in increasing numbers, were temporarily processed at the old Barge Office in Manhattan's Battery Park. Although migration from Europe had been growing steadily in the 1880s, it began to slow in the first few years of the new decade. More restrictive U.S. immigration policies, passed in the spring of 1891, along with a cholera epidemic in 1892 and an economic depression in the mid-1890s, helped reduce the number of newcomers processed at the station in the first few years of its existence. As it turned out, this lull represented the calm before the storm. The old immigration from northern and western Europe had leveled off, but new immigration from southern and eastern Europe had only just begun.

When the new fireproof brick federal immigration station opened on December 17, 1900, nearly twenty-five hundred foreigners seeking residence in America passed through its doors. Not long afterward, that daily rate had almost tripled. The main immigration station building, modeled after the train stations of the era and adorned with hundred-foot (30.5m) towers at the four corners, was nearly the same size as the original: 400 feet long (122m), 165 feet wide (50m), and more than 60 feet (18m) high (two stories). The first floor would be used for baggage, railroad ticket sales, food concessions, and as a waiting room, while the central area of the second floor, later known as the Great Hall, served as the Registry Room and Examination Hall. The second floor also housed the detention areas, special inspection rooms, and administrative offices.

The total cost for the new station—including a restaurant, bath-house, laundry, and dormitory, as well as a hospital completed in 1902—ran to $1.5 million. By 1899, Ellis Island had been expanded to seventeen acres (6.8ha), but still more space was needed. To fill the need, two additional islands were created using landfill: Island Two would house the hospital administration and the contagious diseases ward, and Island Three, built from 1905 to 1906, was to hold the psychiatric ward. Ellis Island, once a mere three acres (1.2ha), had grown to more than twenty-seven acres (11ha). Every inch would be used to hold, process, feed, inspect, and house thousands of people each day during the peak immigration years of 1900 to 1914—numbers far beyond the wildest imaginings of the officials at the new immigration station.

Opposite: A side view of the Barge Office in lower Manhattan between 1897 and 1900. This building served as a temporary immigration-processing center while the new fireproof building on Ellis Island was under construction. The traffic coming from all directions illustrates the level of commotion at this makeshift site.

Above: Constructing the new front wall of the main immigration building, April 1899. This new brick fireproof complex began processing immigrants on December 17, 1900.

Above: Federal inspection officials meet immigrants as they disembark from a transport ferry and move toward the Registry Room to be inspected. The purpose of the inspection was to determine whether an alien had a criminal record, or was a contract laborer, an anarchist, or a polygamist. Inspectors would base their conclusions, in part, on the records they received from the steamship companies, but also on the direct questioning of immigrants at the time of arrival. The information provided by the steamship companies was often sketchy or even inaccurate, since the companies were generally more interested in collecting fees than in gathering accurate information.

Below: The interior of the Great Hall on a typical day. The room was 200 feet (61m) long by 100 feet (30.5m) wide and 56 feet (17.1m) high. In 1916, Spanish immigrant Rafael Guastavino built a sixty-foot-high (18m), barrel-vaulted, tiled ceiling for the hall. Immigrants sat on narrow iron benches until it was their turn to be interrogated by an inspector.

Above: Ellis Island's peak years coincided with the rapid development of Manhattan. The New York City skyline evolved during the first three decades of the twentieth century.

Below: The newly completed immigration station. The press praised the elegant structure, with the *New York Times* calling it a "pleasing addition to the picturesque waterfront of the metropolis." It was estimated that Ellis Island could now handle five thousand people a day—a figure that was reached and surpassed on many a day.

Above: An aerial view of the Statue of Liberty and New York Harbor. Immigrants often recalled their first view of the statue as a particularly transcendent moment after the arduous voyage.

CHAPTER TWO

Journeys

Throughout most of the nineteenth century, Germany, Ireland, Britain, and the Scandinavian countries supplied the vast majority of new immigrants to the United States. By 1890, a dramatic shift began, and although these earlier immigrant groups continued to arrive, newcomers from the Austro-Hungarian Empire, Italy, and Russia began to make up the bulk of those passing through Ellis Island.

Most of these émigrés were desperately poor and many, the Russian Jews and Turkish Armenians in particular, were the victims of religious and political persecution and violence. Some were revolutionaries and others were exiles, but in almost all cases, the mass immigration of the early twentieth century was driven by a sense that life in the Old World offered no hope. In the less developed countries of Europe, especially Poland, Italy, and parts of Greece, industrialization had moved people off the land, and the cities could not provide sufficient employment for most of them. Brutal pogroms and continued economic marginalization within the Pale of Settlement (an area along the western Russian frontier where Jews were confined), brought eastern European Jews to the United States by the millions. Although, in future years, substantial numbers of immigrants moved back and forth between the Old World and the New, the majority of new arrivals in the early twentieth century did not have this option: the United States became their permanent home, and their children were raised as Americans.

The initial long journey to America was extraordinarily difficult for these immigrants, emotionally as well as financially. Although entire families sometimes attempted to take the voyage together, more often one member would make the trip ahead of the rest, find a job, and then begin to save enough money to bring others—ideally the whole family—to the country.

The first family member to enter the country was usually the one considered best suited to becoming a breadwinner in the New World. For many immigrant families, particularly Italians, the pattern of migration adhered to traditional gender roles: the father entered first, after which he would call for the rest of the family to join him, sometimes including extended family members. Among Jewish émigrés, young, unmarried daughters were often considered good candidates for work in the burgeoning garment industry and needle trades, and they frequently made the trip ahead of male family members.

In most instances, preparing for the passage required careful planning and involved major, if not complete, upheaval. Because nearly all of the émigrés lived in rural areas, getting to the port cities of embarkation was costly and required extensive travel. Sicilian immigrant Tony Sabatino, who arrived on Ellis Island in 1900 at age seven, recalled that his family had to first make a two-day, forty-mile (64km) trip to Palermo in a two-wheel cart—which held all six family members, plus a large trunk carrying all their belongings—with one horse and one driver. En route, they slept overnight in a stable, along with the horse. From Palermo, they embarked on a frightening voyage across the choppy Mediterranean to Naples, where they finally boarded the ship that would take them to America.

To finance their journeys, departing family members often had to deal with agents and banks, many of which greedily took advantage of desperate émigrés. Travelers fleeing political oppression faced serious restrictions and were required to secure permits that were often available only in exchange for a sizable bribe. They also had to contend with border patrols. Lithuanian-Jewish immigrant Leon Solomon remembered his family members concealing themselves in a barn and paying intermediaries who specialized in leading immigrants across the Russian-German border illegally; the intermediaries bribed the guards to look away while his family crossed. "At the appropriate moment, when those who were experts in helping emigrants across the border ... thought it was safe, they called to us and said, 'Now run!' " Solomon recalled. "So we picked up our luggage and we ran. And I remember how breathlessly we crossed the border until we were told, 'Stop running!' "

As difficult as their treks through Europe were, for most émigrés these hardships paled in comparison to the long, excruciating sea voyages, often undertaken in steerage or third class and lasting as long as two to three weeks. The Atlantic crossing could be rough even for the wealthier passengers in first or second class. For those making the voyage to New York Harbor in the crowded and unsanitary steerage compartments, the trip was often absolutely miserable. Traveling in steerage literally meant riding near the ship's steering equipment—in essence, like cargo. A typical steerage compartment had no portholes, nor any other form of ventilation; it was unpartitioned and crammed with several tiers of narrow metal bunks topped with paper-thin mattresses.

In such unhealthy quarters, it is not surprising that many immigrants experienced severe seasickness during the passage. Sonya Kevar, raised in Yasinoc, Russia, recalled her twenty-one days on the *Lithuania*: "They had tables for eating but we couldn't eat because we kept throwing up. They didn't give us any medicine. They didn't give us any eggs. Just some kind of meat and soups." The food that these poor travelers most often recount eating, however, was herring—the cheapest commodity available for the ships to serve.

Traveling in steerage also entailed a complete lack of privacy. Shipping companies would jam as many as two thousand immigrants into metal-frame berths in the foul-smelling, low-ceilinged compart-

ments, usually dividing the space into separate dormitories for single women, single men, and families. With almost no bathing or cleaning facilities available, the stench from the human cargo and the ship's galley never abated. Sophia Kreitzberg, a Russian Jew who emigrated in 1908, recalled that "the atmosphere was so thick and dense with smoke and bodily odors that your head itched and when you went to scratch it … you got lice in your hands." The combination of the pounding of the engines and the rocking of the ship on the ocean waves, especially during sudden storms, made recovery from prolonged bouts of seasickness that much more difficult. Many immigrants also remembered getting separated from parents and sometimes not being able to find them for several hours.

Despite these terrible conditions, some of those who traveled as children later recalled getting caught up in the adventure and thrill of the experience, roaming the ship and meeting and making friends with other boys and girls their age. Adult émigrés have also reflected on the kindness of strangers and on chance encounters with fellow travelers who showed generosity and became companions for the duration of the voyage.

By 1910, many ships began to replace steerage with four- and six-berth third-class cabins, but for the poorest passengers, the new arrangement—especially on the older ships—provided only a marginal improvement. These travelers continued to be forced to eat meals

Above: Newcomers wait to disembark from the ferry that has brought them from their steamship to Ellis Island circa 1908. Note that these Jewish immigrants had already received their manifest tags, which gave the name of the ship on which they had arrived.

Above: This group of men and boys is most likely of western Asian ancestry, based on their clothing. Many ethnic groups came to America to escape fierce religious persecution in their homelands.

from tin mess kits while sitting on deck, and although they no longer had to sleep in steerage, the cabins remained cramped and uncomfortable.

Under U.S. immigration law, shipping companies had to meet several conditions in order to be permitted to dock. From 1891 on, these included disinfecting and examining passengers prior to travel, paying for the housing of any detained passengers once they arrived on Ellis Island, and footing the bill for shipping "rejected" immigrants back to their ports of entry. Not surprisingly, the companies complied with the inspection requirements in a cursory manner, preferring to leave it to the American authorities to deal with any medical problems their passengers may have had. A significant number of émigrés who were sent back because of medical ailments may well have been saved the trip if the rules had been followed. Had they been thoroughly inspected before leaving home, they could have made the crossing later, after taking the opportunity to convalesce.

Before sailing, each passenger had to be interrogated by a ship's officer who sought basic information: identification, national origin, destination, financial resources, medical and psychological health, and marital status. Again, the shipping companies were far more interested in pocketing the immigrants' passage fare than in compiling a thorough and accurate manifest log, another reason why the processing at Ellis Island and other ports of entry was often so extensive and time-consuming—as well as intimidating and frightening—for many passengers.

Even after the adversities of travel, however, many immigrants have said that seeing New York Harbor for the first time was one of the most exhilarating and memorable experiences of their lives. The waves and the seasickness were left behind, replaced by feelings of relief, anticipation, and hope. Russian-Jewish immigrant Harriet Kurzweil described the night when her ship arrived in New York: "It was beautiful, all those electric lights." At around "four or five o'clock in the morning," she continued, "we all got up. The whole boat. Everybody came out after such a trip, came out on the boat and facing the shore. The sunshine started, and what do we see? The Statue of Liberty!"

All ships from abroad first stopped in lower New York Harbor, where they stayed pending clearance, and then moved into berths at Manhattan and New Jersey piers. First- and second-class passengers, many of whom were not immigrants, were usually processed on board the ships and allowed to disembark at the berths. Steerage and third-class travelers grabbed their possessions and were transferred to barges that would take them to Ellis Island—their first taste of the New World.

This process could be punishing. Immigrants arrived at a rate of as many as five thousand to ten thousand each day from 1900 to 1914, translating into long lines and overcrowding at the processing station. Sometimes new arrivals had to wait for days aboard their ships before they were transferred to Ellis Island. And even once they reached the island, those immigrants who had sailed third class or in steerage often found themselves confined to barges for hours without food or water, waiting their turn to enter the building for inspection. The barges, chartered by the steamship lines, lacked any form of sanitation facilities, rest rooms, or lifesaving equipment and were oppressively hot in the summer and bitterly cold in the winter. In addition, arriving immigrants had to lug heavy bags and trunks, often containing all their worldly possessions, as they slowly made their way to be processed. It is likely that other newcomers shared the feelings expressed by German immigrant Georg Kruger about being forced to endure the long wait on his ship while first- and second-class passengers moved on: "Isn't it strange that here we are coming to a country where there is complete equality, but not quite so for the newly arrived immigrants?"

Left: Jewish immigrants outside the main building at Ellis Island, circa 1900. Fourteen thousand Jews from Russia and eastern Europe arrived in America in 1880. In 1910, the annual number soared to 484,000, largely as a result of a series of violent pogroms and other political and economic oppression directed against Russian Jews.

Left: Not all immigrants processed on Ellis Island came from Europe. These women entered from Guadalupe, a Caribbean island colonized by the French. Marcus Garvey, leader of the Back to Africa movement, emigrated from Jamaica in 1916 and Harlem Renaissance poet and writer Claude McKay passed through Ellis Island from Trinidad in the early 1920s.

Opposite: Finnish families did not immigrate to the United States in the years prior to World War I. After the war, however, a worsening economic situation in their homeland led approximately eight thousand Finns, such as the family pictured here, to make the trip. This is many fewer than came from Norway, Denmark, and Sweden.

Above: These Montenegrins were part of a new wave of immigrants coming through Ellis Island in the aftermath of World War I. Between 1920 and 1931, twenty-five thousand people left Yugoslavia for America. Thousands of Montenegrins also immigrated to America during the Balkan Wars (1912–1913) against the Turks.

Above: Their long and arduous ocean voyage finally over, a family of Lithuanian immigrants picnics on the deck in front of the immigration station.

Right: An Austrian family, including a newborn, bundled up for a particularly cold day. More than a million immigrants from the Austro-Hungarian Empire came through Ellis Island, making the region the third-largest source of new immigrants, after Italy and Russia, during the peak years of immigration.

Right: A Scandinavian family leaves the transport ferry and takes its first steps onto Ellis Island. Two and a half million immigrants from Scandinavian countries passed through Ellis Island.

Above: This Italian family stands on the deck of one of the small ferries that shuttled newly arrived steerage and third-class passengers from their ships to Ellis Island. Sometimes the number of immigrants was so great that many had to wait several days just to board a ferry to the island.

Left: An engraving from 1892 shows Jewish refugees from Russia passing the Statue of Liberty.

Above: The SS *Adriatic* docks at the Ellis Island port in July 1923. After immigration quotas were enacted in 1921, there was frenzied competition among ships to determine which ones would be permitted to dock, based on whether that particular country had exceeded its monthly quota.

Left: Ferries like this one were used by the Immigration Service to move immigrants from their ships to Ellis Island. Only passengers sailing in third class or steerage, on the very lowest level of the ships, were required to pass through the immigration station. First- and second-class travelers were processed quickly onboard and permitted to disembark in Manhattan.

Above: Having been successfully processed, these lucky immigrants are being escorted from the ferry to the mainland. After leaving the island, about one-third of the newcomers took the ferry to the Battery in Manhattan. The others went by barge to a railroad station in Hoboken or Jersey City, New Jersey, where they continued to other destinations in the United States.

Above: Young boys shoulder the heavy bags and bundles that this family brought to the New World.

Above: An immigrant family on Ellis Island gazes across New York Harbor at the Statue of Liberty, which for many was the symbol of America. The statue, a gift from the people of France in 1886, was a new addition to the harbor when the immigration station opened in 1892.

Above: A German family receives tags marked with their final destination for a railroad trip out of the Port of New York. From 1820, more than seventy years before the opening of the immigration station at Ellis Island, to 1938, nearly six million Germans came to the United States. German immigration declined after 1890, but it still added up to the highest number of newcomers to America from any one country.

Above: A Dutch woman and her eleven children line up in front of one of the hospital buildings. This family eventually settled in Minnesota. Immigrants who passed through Ellis Island as children usually preserved vivid memories of the experience.

Above: On an especially foggy day on Ellis Island, a man points out the Statue of Liberty to his son.

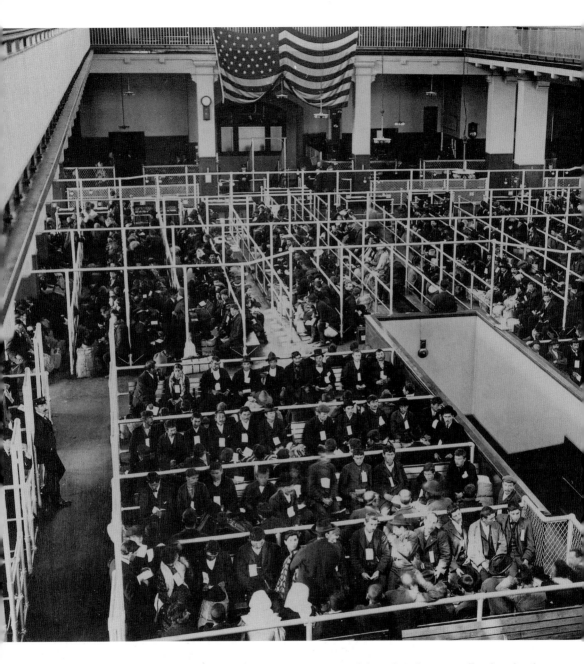

Above: The packed quarters in the main Registry Room on a typical day. The white tags affixed to the chests of the immigrants are manifest cards, on which was recorded a number corresponding to the order in which each immigrant was listed on the ship's registry. The cards were filled out by the steamship companies and handed over to immigration officials at disembarkation.

Below: A family of Serbian Gypsies poses in front of the immigration station. Gypsies were often suspected of being professional beggars and vagabonds. As a result, they faced discrimination from immigration inspectors, who were especially vigilant about making sure they had money. Large families like this one also had the difficult task of staying together amidst the crowds and confusion that often accompanied the examination process.

Below: This drawing by G.W. Peters depicts a volunteer serving soup to immigrants on the roof garden of Ellis Island's main building. Representatives from organizations such as the Hebrew Immigrant Aid Society, the Italian Welfare League, the Catholic Welfare Council, and the Daughters of the American Revolution all worked at Ellis Island on behalf of immigrants.

Left: Clutching their belongings, a group of women leaves the Ellis Island processing station. Many immigrants left their home countries with the expectation that they would never return. As a result, they packed their most valued possessions in bags and baskets for the long voyage to America.

Right: This 1907 photograph by Alfred Stieglitz shows a view of the packed quarters of a transatlantic ship, with passengers riding in steerage down below.

Left: During peak years, as vast numbers of immigrants poured in daily, the facility often had difficulty accommodating newcomers as soon as they arrived, and many were forced to remain outside until space became available. In addition, the ferries were not always able to conform to the schedules of immigration officials, so immigrants sometimes arrived on the island before or after regular business hours and had to wait until the building opened for the day.

Left: Italian immigrants like those pictured here came mostly from impoverished southern Italy and Sicily, and made up by far the largest number of any ethnic group entering the United States through Ellis Island, totaling more than two and a half million. Although Italian immigrants quickly became important members of the American cultural mix, there was enormous prejudice against them during the early years of the twentieth century.

Above: Immigrants leaving Ellis Island to begin their new lives in America. For the approximately 80 percent who were able to successfully fulfill the requirements of the inspection, processing on the island could be as short as three hours. Others who were not so lucky could be detained for days or weeks, depending on the circumstances.

CHAPTER THREE

The Teeming Masses

The name "Island of Hope, Island of Tears" reflected the extraordinary diversity of the immigrant experience on Ellis Island. For many individuals and families who were in good health, had their papers in order, and were able to pass smoothly through the medical and legal inspections, the process could take as little as three to five hours, after which they were free to begin their new lives. That accomplishment, especially when it involved a reunion with family members already in the United States, was truly a cause for celebration and made Ellis Island a gateway of hope—the final, joyful step in a journey that had taken months and perhaps years of planning.

Nonetheless, the examination procedure was often humiliating and frightening, even for the vast majority of immigrants who eventually made it through successfully. Inspection officials could be accommodating and even gentle with the newcomers, but due to the massive numbers of individuals being processed, their treatment of immigrants was often brusque and aggressive at best, and downright hostile at worst. For the small but significant minority who were detained—up to 20 percent during the peak years of immigration—the station could indeed be an "Island of Tears." Detainees' stays could last as long as several days or even several weeks. And for the 2 percent ordered to return to their home countries, the "Island of Tears" could well be described as the "Island of their Worst Nightmares."

Prior to landing, immigrants received tags, which were pinned to their clothing, indicating their ship name and manifest number. This number corresponded to the ship's manifest log, which listed each immigrant's name and his or her answers to twenty-nine questions. The new arrivals were then ordered to line up in numerical order under the canopy in front of the main building, and were eventually led inside. The queue, which often stretched all the way from the dock to the baggage room, then wound its way up the main stairway to the second floor, where, until 1911, the medical examinations took place. As each person moved up in the line, the public health doctors working at the inspection station were already beginning their examinations, looking to see who was coughing or walking with a limp or rubbing their eyes as they ascended into the Great Hall, the central examining area.

At the top of the stairs, immigrants moved in single file past two doctors, who were spaced far enough apart to study the newcomers as they walked. The official medical examination involved checking for more than sixty diseases, symptoms, and disabilities that might be grounds to deny entry. Because they were attempting to check as many as five thousand immigrants in the course of a day, physicians spent no more than two minutes with each person and often even less. Examiners were especially concerned with finding contagious diseases, such as cholera, malaria, favus (scalp and nail fungus), and trachoma, a highly contagious eye condition that caused the most detentions and deportations among immigrants. They also looked for signs of partial blindness or deafness and any mental or emotional impairment. In 1907, when stricter medical restrictions were put into effect, epilepsy, mental deficiency, physical disability, and tuberculosis became causes to detain immigrants.

If, in the process of observing the hands, face, and throat of an immigrant as he or she approached, physicians saw any reason for further examination, they would put a chalk mark on the person's back or chest, based on a letter code developed by medical inspectors. Roughly 20 percent of all immigrants received these marks, a likely source of tremendous anxiety and fear. The rather mystifying code included Pg for pregnant, K for hernia, and Ft for feet. Those suspected of being mentally infirm received a mark of X. Immigrants with chalk marks were taken out of the line and led to special examination rooms, where a doctor checked them for the illness in question and then gave them a short overall physical. They were then held in screened detention areas—similar to large cages and visible to other immigrants—and later moved to either special inspection areas for further examination, bathhouses for disinfecting, or the hospital for observation and care. New arrivals determined to have incurable or disabling ailments faced the prospect of being sent back to their ports of origin.

After the first cursory inspection, each person received a closer examination for trachoma. Using a buttonhook to turn each immigrant's eyelid inside out, physicians checked for inflammation. Immigrant after immigrant reported on this painful and terrifying procedure, and the "buttonhook men" earned a reputation as perhaps the most dreaded doctors on Ellis Island. Russian-Jewish émigré Fannie Kligerman remembered that one of her brothers had an eye infection and the family feared it would cause them all to be deported. Her mother had to sign a release giving permission for officials to take her brother away to try to cure him, which they eventually did. Nonetheless, she recounted, "This I remember well—the eye exam. It was such a fright, such a fright."

Immigrants marked with an X during the line inspection were forced to undergo an extensive process known as "mental testing." During that era, people deemed to be of "feeble mind" were deeply stigmatized, and the Immigration Act of 1892 officially barred "idiots" and "lunatics." Newcomers were entering a country with little more sympathy or concern for the nuances of mental health than the places they had left behind.

Approximately nine out of every one hundred immigrants ended up being detained for mental examinations and further questioning. Usually, the testing took the form of simple arithmetic problems or puzzles. Because of language and cultural barriers, Ellis Island doctors tried to create examinations that focused on problem solving and did not have to be explained by an interpreter or require that the immigrant be able to read and write. Nevertheless, these were hardly scientific methods for determining mental fitness. Future New York City mayor Fiorello La Guardia, who worked as an interpreter for the Immigration Service at Ellis Island from 1907 until 1910 while completing law school, was convinced that more than half of the deportations for mental illness were unjustified, oftentimes due more to the ignorance of the doctors than to the alleged feeblemindedness of the immigrant.

Following passage through the medical examination area, immigrants moved to the Great Hall, also known as the Registry Room, a space likened by many to the Tower of Babel because of the noisy crescendo of different languages echoing against the walls and high ceiling. The scene must have been overwhelming, with people of many nations intermingled, not knowing quite where they were or what kinds of questions they would be asked, and hoping that the responses they gave would be the ones the authorities wanted to hear. They waited here—often for a long time—until the call came for the legal inspection.

Below: An immigration service ferry deposits its load of trunks and suitcases on Ellis Island. Ferry crews would sometimes unload the luggage for passengers to pick up after disembarkation.

Upon receiving notice, newcomers, alone or as a family, were peppered with questions from immigration officials to determine their social, economic, and moral fitness. Immigrants were asked about their marital status, work history, prospects for employment, and criminal records. Newly arriving foreigners had to show that they had twenty-five dollars' worth of currency before they could leave the island—an enormous sum for a large family. For many, the interrogation served as the final stop prior to leaving the island, but for an unlucky minority, it meant being detained for a legal hearing. The legal inspection was where immigrants' names were often changed or shortened, perhaps due to the difficulties of reading the handwritten ship manifest ledgers or the inability of a passenger to make himself understood.

Corruption and the exploitation of vulnerable newcomers by unscrupulous immigration officials and agents continued to plague the system in the early years of Ellis Island. Inspectors sometimes demanded bribes from immigrants before they would allow them to pass their examinations, and would have them detained if they did not have the money. Other officials admitted attractive young women in exchange for sexual favors. Railroad agents sold tickets at increased prices. Money-changing employees lied about exchange rates and pocketed the difference. Some immigration officials were even found guilty of issuing phony certificates of citizenship for a fee and then dividing the profits with ship officers. Though the graft and corruption at Ellis Island was an improvement over the blatant thievery of Castle Garden, it still left a lot to be desired.

The Progressive Era ushered in a new reform agenda in America and a new commissioner of immigration, William Williams, was appointed by Theodore Roosevelt to clean up Ellis Island. Williams eliminated corruption in contracts for money-changing, food, and baggage concessions and, in an effort to ensure that immigrants were treated courteously, began enforcing regulations on proper codes of conduct. Like many Americans of his day, however, Williams held ambivalent attitudes toward immigration. On the one hand, he believed in weeding out criminality and improving the conditions of the poor. On the other hand, he supported a strict racial hierarchy that favored Anglo-Saxon immigrants from Germany and England, and enforced the twenty-five-dollar entry fee as a means of keeping out what he called "low-grade immigrants" from southern and eastern Europe. In 1914, another reformer, Commissioner of Immigration Frederic Howe, appointed by Democratic president Woodrow Wilson, repealed the twenty-five-dollar rule, created additional outdoor space for recreational use, and eliminated some of the railings and bars to make moving through the inspection process more humane.

After the legal inspection, immigrants were led from the Registry Room down what was known as the "Stairs of Separation," which, for the majority, meant joyous reunions with family members who

were meeting them on the other side of the fence. Upon positive identification by the sponsor, each newcomer was released to this person's custody. Those without a sponsor were cleared only if they could prove that they could support themselves without becoming public charges. Because many families had been separated for years, the identification was sometimes difficult. Sonya Kevar remembered that when her father came to meet the family, "I couldn't recognize him.... He was dressed like an American." But usually the initial confusion soon gave way to extraordinary happiness as wives were reunited with husbands they hadn't seen in years and fathers met children they had left behind as infants.

For the one in five immigrants being detained during the peak years, the "Stairs of Separation" meant that they would be left behind while others began their lives in America. In 1907, Ellis Island's peak immigration year, nearly 200,000 people were detained for some length of time. All they could do was wait … and hope.

Above: A sweeping view of New York Harbor and the Statue of Liberty. Newcomers were always amazed by their first glimpse of "Lady Liberty."

Right: A woman from southern Europe clutches her precious documents as she leaves the Ellis Island ferry.

Left: Immigrant families disembark from the shuttle ferry, setting foot on American soil for the first time. As they entered the main floor of the building, new arrivals were permitted to leave their baggage in storage while they went through the inspection process.

Below: Decked out in their finest clothes, a family of German immigrants arrives on Ellis Island filled with hope and anticipation.

Above: The crowded deck of a transatlantic ship bound for America. The ship's officers (right, center) appear to be asking the passengers for their papers or identification.

Above: Immigrants were channeled into lines to wait to see the medical examiner. For those with visible illnesses, the medical inspection was the most dreaded part of the Ellis Island process, as the detection of an infectious disease could result in deportation. In the initial medical inspection, which lasted no more than two minutes, immigrants suspected of having a disease or a disability received a coded chalk mark on their back or chest: B for back problems, C for conjunctivitis, Ct for trachoma, and so on. Immigrants who received marks were detained in large caged areas while they awaited a closer examination.

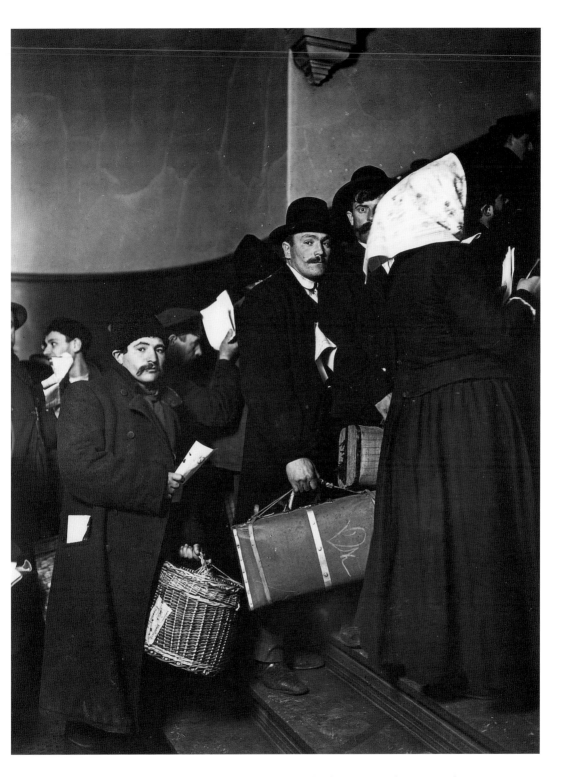

Above: Slavic immigrants clutch their official papers as they make their way up the stairs to the Registry Room, where they will begin their medical inspection.

Above: The main hospital at Ellis Island had its own dispensary for the distribution and storage of medicines and medical supplies.

Right: During the medical-inspection procedure, men stripped to the waist and walked single file past inspectors who identified those in need of further examination. The men who were singled out would then be pulled out of the line for individual attention from public-health physicians.

Above: A glimpse of the men's section of the medical examination room. After 1911, medical exams were conducted on the ground floor of the inspection building. Because of the enormous volume of immigrant traffic, only those who were suspected of having disabilities or infectious diseases received the kind of individual attention that is depicted here.

Above: Intelligence tests were supposedly intended to weed out immigrants who had mental deficiencies. In an era when eugenics was on the rise, the highly subjective and unscientific tests administered on Ellis Island were considered legitimate mechanisms to deny entry to the "feebleminded." In 1917, literacy tests became another tool to limit immigration. All immigrants aged sixteen and older were required to read a forty-word passage, often a translation from the Bible, in their native language.

Right: An immigrant undergoes a psychological examination. Any mental deficiencies discovered in this process could result in the denial of entry into the United States. After 1917, immigrants could also be deported for the inability to read in English or in their native language.

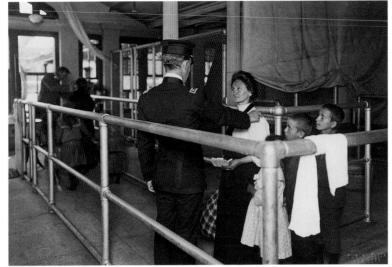

Left: Children line up behind their mother for the medical inspection. In the background, a doctor appears to be checking a child's eyes, most likely for trachoma, the most common medical reason for detention and deportation. Identification of any infectious disease by a medical examiner could be grounds for denial of entry.

Above: A woman receives the most painful part of the medical inspection, the test for trachoma, which involved turning the eyelid inside out with a buttonhook to look for inflammation. Inspectors also looked for scabs under the eyelids, a sign of conjunctivitis.

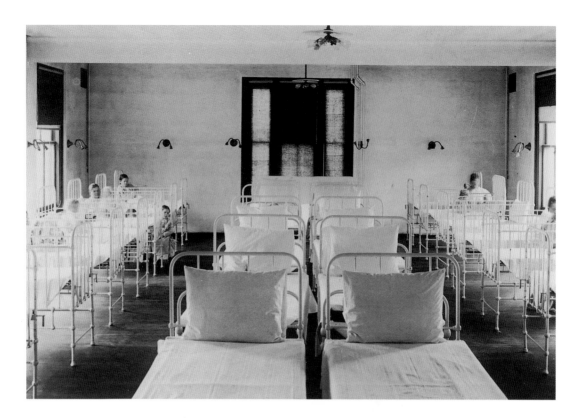

Above: The massive volume of immigrants tested Ellis Island's capacity to provide adequate medical care. A 125-bed hospital was completed in 1902 and then expanded in 1907 and 1910. By 1911, more than fifteen buildings on the island were used strictly for medical care, including a 450-bed contagious-disease ward and a psychiatric ward.

Above: An inspector questions an immigrant during an examination. Immigration officials wielded awesome power over prospective new Americans. Their decisions often determined if Ellis Island would be an "island of hope" or an "island of tears" for a particular immigrant.

Above: With the addition of Island Two and Island Three, which housed hospital wards and administration offices, the original three-acre (1.2ha) island was increased to twenty-seven acres (10.9ha). Buildings such as this one were added to accommodate the increasing number of immigrants.

Above: This looks like a rather friendly interaction between an immigrant woman and a physician. Although the station often earned its reputation for treating newcomers no better than animals, many inspectors showed great understanding and sensitivity toward the plight of those who were making their way through an often intimidating process.

Above: A woman is interrogated during the legal inspection as others look on anxiously. The legal inspectors, who were particularly concerned that immigrants would become public charges or be hired as contract laborers, had real authority to detain and deport, unlike the public-health physicians, who could only make recommendations and provide supporting evidence.

Below: An extended immigrant family with an infant. Immigration officials sometimes detained pregnant women traveling alone if they suspected that the child might not have adequate financial support and that both mother and child would become public charges. Although women who were more than five months pregnant were typically not allowed to emigrate from their home countries, a number of births occurred on Ellis Island.

Opposite: Italian immigrants looking for lost luggage in 1905. At the height of immigration, the ground floor of the main building was used for storing baggage. Eight decades after this photograph was taken, this family was identified as Anna Sciacchitano and her children, Paul, Mary, and Dominick. Anna had immigrated with her children to join her husband, Giovanni, in Scranton, Pennsylvania.

Above: The crowded women's section of the dining hall. As the immigrant population increased in the first decade of the twentieth century, kitchens were forced to serve meals all day long. Men and women were separated in the dining room. Children under twelve ate with their mothers, while older boys and girls could eat with either parent.

Above: The long view of the dining area set up for lunch. There was little variation in the meals but the food was plentiful. A typical day's menu would offer a breakfast of bread with butter and coffee with milk and sugar, a lunch of beef stew, potatoes, rye bread, and herring, and for supper, baked beans, stewed prunes, bread, and tea with milk and sugar. A kosher kitchen, which prepared separate meals for Jewish immigrants, was added in 1911.

Above: The bakery at Ellis Island. One thing immigrants seemed to agree on was that there was plenty of food available at the station, although opinion was divided as to its quality and the sanitary conditions of the dining and other food-service facilities.

Right: Bohemian and Bulgarian men and boys enjoy a Christmas dinner in the men's area of the dining room, which has been decorated with garlands of greenery for the occasion.

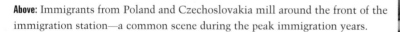

Above: Immigrants from Poland and Czechoslovakia mill around the front of the immigration station—a common scene during the peak immigration years.

Above: Children rest outside the main immigration building. With the extraordinary crowding inside, many detainees, especially children, found that the outdoor recreation areas offered some relief.

Above: A view of the roof garden on the west wing of the Main Building, one of several outdoor spaces that immigrants were permitted to use for recreation and fresh air while they were in detention. Recreation areas like this one were some of the few places where detained women and men could interact more freely and where children could enjoy the fresh air and have a place to play.

Below: The comfortably furnished Red Cross House, located on Island Two, was built in the first decade of the twentieth century to accommodate emergency medical personnel. It was torn down in 1923.

Right: A throng of new immigrants waits to exchange money. This photograph, taken after World War I, shows the number of arrivals on the rise again after a drop during the war years.

Above: The Railroad Ticket Office at Ellis Island. Newcomers who had passed inspection could purchase tickets to a number of different destinations. After arranging travel plans, they received tags to wear on their hats or coats showing railroad conductors the lines on which they were traveling and the connections they needed to make. Although roughly one-third of immigrants remained in New York City, many traveled to other cities, often to join family members who had already settled in the area.

Opposite, bottom: Exchanging their money was an important step for immigrants. Among other expenses, they were required to pay the rail companies for tickets after they were processed on the island. The exchange was also a source of rampant corruption, as unscrupulous agents shortchanged vulnerable immigrants and then pocketed the difference. One of Commissioner Williams's reform efforts was an attempt to crack down on this practice.

Above: Family reunions after the examination process were scenes of tremendous joy. Immigrants bound for Manhattan met relatives at a spot that became known as "the kissing post," which was also the site of many weddings.

Above: After inspection, immigrants proceeded down what were referred to as the "Stairs of Separation," dividing those who were free to leave the island from those who would be detained for an indefinite time. The majority of immigrants proceeded to either the Railroad Ticket Office or the ferry that would take them to the Battery in Manhattan. The less fortunate went either to the island's detention room or to its hospital.

Above: Cleared to proceed, a group of immigrants leaves Ellis Island behind them as they walk toward the ferries that will take them to Battery Park.

Right: The waiting was not over with the completion of the inspection process. Here immigrants who have passed through the entry station at Ellis Island wait in a long line for the ferry to Manhattan.

Above: A number of young women traveled to the New World to be married. The immigration authorities tended to treat these newcomers with suspicion. Some of the women were sent to America by marriage brokers in southern and eastern Europe to meet young European men who had settled in the United States and wanted to marry women from their home countries. These women were often referred to as "picture brides" because the men and women exchanged photographs prior to meeting one another.

CHAPTER FOUR

Are We Home Yet?

The decision to immigrate to the United States often involved tremendous physical, emotional, and financial risk. People sold property and left behind valued friends, jobs, and most of their possessions in order to make the long trip. So when the anticipated entry to America did not occur as expected and an immigrant faced the prospect of being detained on Ellis Island, the experience was traumatic.

The reasons for being denied entry included: medical problems, mental illness, a criminal record, the likelihood of becoming a public charge, and being a contract laborer—someone imported by an employer or an agent of that employer strictly to work. Children under the age of sixteen unaccompanied by an adult were always held for special inquiry, as were stowaways and alien seamen. After 1917, illiteracy—the inability to read in English or one's native language—also became a cause for detention, as did the possibility of being imported into "white slavery," or prostitution.

Most people were detained for a relatively short time while they received medical attention or waited for money to arrive or a relative to meet them. Some, however, had to spend days or even weeks in cramped, crowded conditions before they finally passed through the "golden doors." Although only 2 percent suffered the saddest fate—being sent back to their countries of origin—this still translated to one thousand refusals a month during the peak years.

Young, unmarried women who traveled unescorted regularly encountered difficulties trying to pass through Ellis Island. Immigration inspectors claimed that young women with limited skills and resources were in danger of becoming destitute or being sold into prostitution by hustlers, and thus detained them, supposedly for their own protection. These women were not allowed to leave the island alone or with any man not related to them. They could be released unescorted only after they received a telegram, letter, or prepaid ticket to their final destinations from a relative or a recognized social-service organization. Fiancées nearly always had to be met by their husbands-to-be and then married on the spot, in the presence of immigration officials, to be allowed to proceed into the country. Unescorted women who did not meet these requirements risked being sent back to their ports of origin. Pregnant women traveling alone could also be refused entry if officials believed that the mother and child might become wards of the state. Although some of these strictures were undoubtedly inspired by real dangers, discrimination against women certainly played a role. Much of the "white slavery" scare was fueled by a turn-of-the-century national hysteria—a purity crusade—that overstated the severity of the problem and was used to limit the freedom of the women it claimed to be protecting.

Immigrants held for nonmedical reasons were brought before one of several boards of special inquiry, consisting of three immigration inspectors who heard each case privately and made their decisions based solely on the evidence presented by the individual. Detainees had no counsel or right to a jury trial, but they did have access to interpreters and could call witnesses, usually relatives, to help make their case. They were also allowed to appeal the decision. In order to win their case, immigrants had to convince officials that they had adequate financial support or show documentation proving that immediate family members or other relatives could vouch for them. Among the most difficult challenges for detainees going before the board was persuading officials that they had good prospects for work while also verifying that they had not been hired as contract laborers.

Another major reason for detention was an immigrant's inability to provide the certificates that proved he did not have a criminal record. When this happened, officials often considered detainees guilty until proven innocent. Mayor Fiorello La Guardia, who had once worked at Ellis Island, believed that many immigrants were being deported unfairly, either for minor offenses or because their certificates had been translated inaccurately. Thanks to the work of reformers such as La Guardia and the many social-welfare organizations that came to the aid of immigrants, these flaws in the detention process were challenged, and many people who might otherwise have been denied entry received the assistance they needed to enter the United States. Helen Barth of the Hebrew Immigrant Aid Society (HIAS), one of the most important of these agencies, reflected on the group's responsibilities: "We saw these people through by helping them. We took care of their health, we gave them food, we gave them clothing, we gave them homes, and we had representatives going all up and down the East Coast, speaking to all kinds of groups to employ these thousands of people, who were without funds."

By providing detention cases with translation services, financial support, and legal advocacy, groups such as HIAS, the Italian Welfare League, the Polish Society, the Travelers' Aid Society, and the Immigrants Protective League acted as saviors for hundreds of Ellis Island detainees. Largely as a result of the work of these agencies, the vast majority of detained immigrants eventually received clearance to begin their new lives in America. Other detainees had to rely on their relatives, benevolent examiners, or their own guile and brains to win the support of the boards. Boards reviewed as many as seventy thousand cases a year, and, ultimately, five out of six detainees whose cases were heard by these inspectors were admitted into the country. Detainees who were rejected could appeal their cases directly to the Secretary of Commerce and Labor, and at that time they could hire an attorney.

Whether long or short, the detention itself was almost invariably a difficult and demoralizing experience. Because of the extreme space

limitations, Ellis Island authorities housed detainees in makeshift dormitories: two long, narrow, sex-segregated rooms along both sides of the Registry Room mezzanine. Each room, created by installing wire gates, slept three hundred people in narrow, triple-tiered bunks with no mattresses. Nor were there pillows or sheets, and the space between each tier was no more than two feet (0.6m). The gates were raised each morning so that the space could be converted back into a daytime waiting area. Ventilation was virtually nonexistent, making sleeping and living arrangements that much more miserable during hot summer months. Bathhouses were equipped to handle only two hundred people per day. Detainees complained about chronic lice problems and the generally unsanitary conditions in the building. In many ways, detention differed little from traveling steerage on a ship, but at least on Ellis Island immigrants did not have to worry about becoming seasick.

Despite the beneficence and goodwill of a number of inspectors, detainees frequently reported being herded into cages, bullied, and threatened with deportation by Ellis Island employees. Armenian immigrant Marta Kazarian, who spent three and a half weeks in detention, recalled, "They [Ellis Island employees] pushed you around. They pushed you into showers—burning hot water … It was either too hot or too cold, they didn't care. So you got out and they pushed two blankets into your arms and they pushed you into a room, bare cots, one blanket under you, one blanket on top of you, and that was your bed."

In cases of medical detention, family members could be separated from one another, sometimes for long periods. Armenian immigrant Jeanne Assidian remembered taking care of two sisters and a brother while her parents were hospitalized for eye problems: "It was very lonely without our parents for two weeks. We didn't see them at all. We knew that they were in the hospital and that's about all." M. Gertrude Slaughter, who served as a public-health physician on Ellis Island in the 1920s, recalled an emotional incident in which the mother of a child infected with scarlet fever panicked and attacked attendants when they tried to take the child to the infectious disease ward. "She thought her child was being taken away forever." Once a translator could be found to explain the situation, the woman calmed down.

Approximately 98 percent of immigrants who passed through Ellis Island were, however, eventually allowed through the golden doors. Sick parents and children recovered, relatives sent the necessary money or official letters of support, and legal concerns were resolved. The unlucky 2 percent were sent back across the ocean, their long journeys having been in vain.

During the peak immigration years, more than 200,000 people were denied entry to the United States. Among those deported were people deemed to have contagious illnesses that could not be cured. Others were accused of being criminals or of filing fraudulent applications. After 1917, mental illness or failure to pass the literacy test

could also be used as grounds to permanently bar an immigrant from proceeding further into America.

In the years leading up to World War I and during the "Red Scare" that followed, decisions about who could and could not enter the country became entangled in larger political battles over immigration policy in the United States. Commissioner of Immigration Frederic Howe put it succinctly when he said, "The whole country was swept by emotional excesses that followed one another with confusing swiftness from 1916 to 1920."

Above: Exhausted immigrants rest on the lawn in front of the main building. This image reveals the physical toll taken by the long voyage to America.

Above: An immigrant woman being questioned by an Ellis Island inspector. The other woman at the table is most likely a translator. During the peak immigration years, translators were hired to assist with the processing of newcomers. Among the most famous was future New York City mayor Fiorello La Guardia, who worked as an interpreter from 1907 to 1910, while he attended law school. He believed that many immigrants detained as "mentally deficient" were misdiagnosed due to communication problems between the individual and the doctor.

Left: Women traveling alone were automatically detained at Ellis Island until a family member came to escort them onto the mainland or until they received a telegram, letter, or prepaid ticket from a relative.

Right: Immigrants held by inspectors for nonmedical reasons were brought before boards of special inquiry. Most often, their money had not arrived or they lacked sponsors and were perceived as risks of becoming public charges. Others were held because they were suspected of having criminal records or of being contract laborers or prostitutes, anarchists or polygamists. The boards of special inquiry consisted of three immigration officials, who heard the cases and rendered their decisions based on the evidence presented. The immigrant had no right to counsel but did have the services of an interpreter and was sometimes allowed to call witnesses.

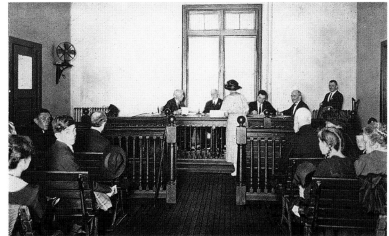

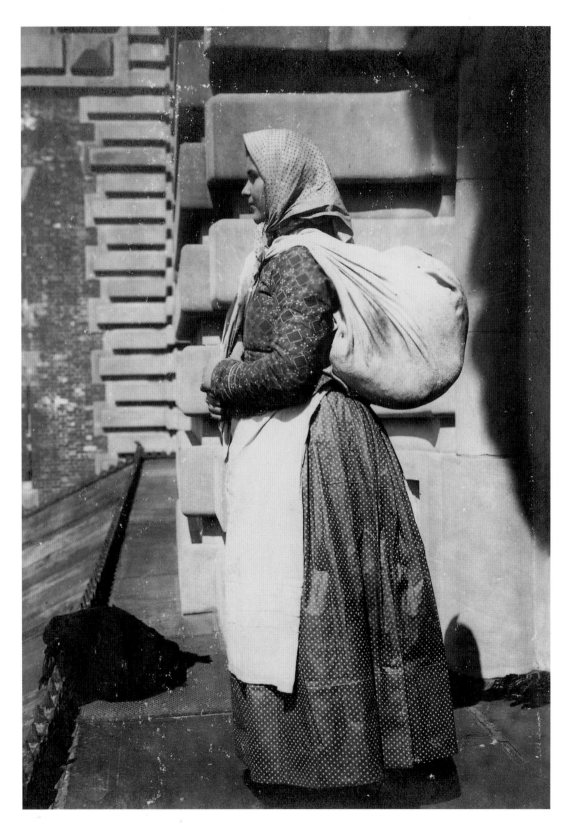

Opposite: Judging by her ker-
chief—or babushka—and
sack, this woman probably
came from eastern Europe,
most likely Russia, Hungary,
Poland, or Slovakia.

Above: This image captures part of the "Americanization" process on Ellis Island. Classes on the island stressed good citizenship and the notion that the children should now consider themselves American.

Below: A 1918 photograph of Cecilia Greenstone of the National Council of Jewish Women. Many observers have claimed that thousands of families might have been deported were it not for the efforts of social workers such as Greenstone. At a gathering to mark her seventy-fifth birthday in 1962, Cecilia Greenstone Arnow reflected that her work on Ellis Island had been "to rescue human dignity from this nightmare—that was the single thought that my co-workers and I had. To show them that in all the hard sorrow of their lives, they did not stand alone."

Above: The Registry Room in 1912. This room was later adorned with a magnificent barrel-vaulted ceiling by Rafael Guastavino.

Below: One of the most disturbing aspects of Ellis Island history is the number of people who became seriously ill or died while in detention. During the peak immigration years, the station's hospital beds were frequently packed to capacity, and the overworked hospital staff struggled to care for children suffering from measles, scarlet fever, and diphtheria. Hospital buildings and disease wards were rapidly constructed between 1900 and 1915 to meet the growing need for medical care.

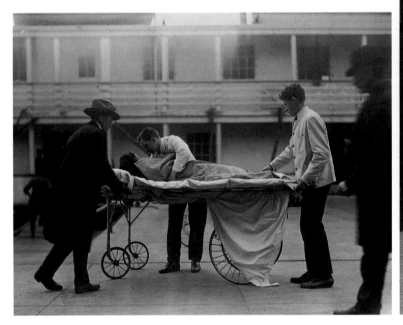

Above: Although detainees were given meals free of charge, immigrants could also purchase food, either to eat while they waited or to take with them on their journeys, from private concessions such as this one.

Left: On the crowded recreation deck in front of the main building, adults stretch their legs while children pass the time playing games. Reformer and commisioner of immigration Fredric Howe created new outdoor areas for detained immigrants. Although this image gives the feeling of people clustered in a large cage, the fresh air on the deck came as a welcome relief after being cooped up indoors.

Above: During the "Red Scare" following World War I, Ellis Island was used to intern immigrant radicals accused of subversive activity. This photo shows accused radicals who have just arrived at the station.

Left: To ease the tedium of detention, these immigrant women formed an impromptu embroidery circle in the first-floor waiting area of the station.

Above: A kindergarten class enjoys the fresh air at one of Commissioner Howe's playgrounds in 1925.

Above: Twenty percent of the immigrants passing through Ellis Island were detained for anywhere from two hours to a few weeks. The process took a physical and emotional toll on individuals and families.

Above: Many of the most poignant Ellis Island stories are those recounted by immigrants who arrived in America as children. Some tell of being separated from their parents for long periods while the adults received medical treatment.

Above: A young Italian boy with his baggage.

Above: These women have purchased two packages of food for the trip to their final destinations. The tags pinned to their coats indicate which trains they need to take.

CHAPTER FIVE

The Closing of the Golden Doors

World War I began in Europe in 1914. By 1916, Ellis Island's mission became twofold: to evaluate the fitness of immigrants seeking to enter the United States and to be the hub for detaining suspected enemy aliens. All over the country, immigrants were arrested for alleged prostitution and other charges related to "white slavery," which was believed to be under the control of a secret network of aliens residing in the United States. Hundreds charged with these crimes were detained on Ellis Island.

When the United States entered the war in 1917, anti-immigrant sentiment intensified. The belief that immigrants represented a threat to American security and safety became widespread, and the foreign-born were denounced as racially inferior, radical subversives who imported crime, poverty, immorality, and disease. Approximately eighteen hundred German citizens were seized on ships at various East Coast ports and then interned at Ellis Island to await deportation. The Department of Justice also ordered the arrests of thousands of other aliens suspected of subversion and the undermining of the U.S. war effort. They were also taken to Ellis Island. A disgruntled Commissioner Howe observed in 1918 that he had become more of a jailer than a commissioner of immigration.

During World War I, immigration declined dramatically. With Atlantic ports and shipping lanes closed to commercial traffic and the country in no mood to welcome foreigners, the number of newcomers entering Ellis Island fell from 178,000 in 1915 to less than 150,000 in 1916 and 1917 to a low of 26,000 in 1919. Immediately following the Allied victory in Europe, the United States experienced a massive Red Scare, which arose in the aftermath of the Russian Revolution. Under the direction of Attorney General A. Mitchell Palmer, thousands of communists, anarchists, and other radicals— U.S. citizens and foreign-born aliens alike—were arrested and prosecuted in trials with virtually no rights of due process. The aliens were sent to Ellis Island for internment or deportation. Although the resistance that emerged from reformers like Howe prevented a number of deportations from being carried out, the government succeeded in banishing many radicals from its shores, the most famous being the anarchists Emma Goldman and Alexander Berkman. Howe himself became a victim of this crusade and was pressured into resigning his post in 1919.

By 1920, with wartime hysteria fading into the background, immigration through Ellis Island was on the rise again, reaching prewar numbers of 560,000 in 1921. But conditions at the station may have been worse in the 1920s than during the prior decade. The army had used the Registry Room as a ward for wounded servicemen during the war, and the floors and walls were badly in need of repair. Staff who had been laid off during the war had not been replaced; thus the resources available to process immigrants were woefully inadequate. And although the number of newcomers was increasing, anti-immigrant feelings continued to seethe.

In 1921, Republican president Warren Harding signed the first Immigrant Quota Act, effectively ending the Open Door policy that had existed, at least under federal law, by setting limits on the number of immigrants the United States would accept from a given country. By stipulating that annual immigration from a country could not exceed 3 percent of the total number of immigrants from that nation residing in the United States in 1910, this act made it far more difficult for people from southern and eastern Europe to enter the country. Thus, the Quota Act was not simply anti-immigrant, it was an attempt to ensure that white, Protestant, northern Europeans would make up the bulk of newcomers, and that immigration from southern and eastern Europe would be drastically limited. Nonetheless, this policy did not go far enough for the restrictionists in Congress, who escalated their rhetoric about the dangers of the "melting pot":

Below: From this view, the main building on Ellis Island resembles a Venetian palazzo.

immigrants, including those from the "less desirable" countries, continued to enter Ellis Island each year in the hundreds of thousands.

The 1924 National Origins Act went a giant step further than the quota law enacted three years earlier. This act limited total annual immigration to 165,000 and established a national-origins system, fixing quotas of roughly 66,000 from Great Britain, 26,000 from Germany, 6,000 from Italy, and 2,700 from Russia, among others. In addition, the act increased the severity of penalties for steamship companies "found guilty of bringing aliens to this country who are not admissible." The numbers passing through Ellis Island went down and stayed at this low level throughout the next decade. The era of mass immigration into the Port of New York was over.

Above: This aerial view from the northeast shows that Ellis Island was, in fact, three contiguous islands, joined together by landfill taken from the excavation of Grand Central Station and subway tunnels.

Opposite: A group of immigrants pass their time in detention with music and dance. The sign on the wall reads "No charge for meals here" in six different languages.

Above: A Czechoslovak grandmother, 1926. Until the nation of Czechoslovakia was created in 1918, immigrants from the region were differentiated between the primarily Protestant Czechs and the generally Catholic Slovaks so that today there are twice as many Czechs in the United States as there are Slovaks.

Above: This Armenian Jew, photographed in 1926, most likely fled his native land to escape Turkish persecution after World War I.

Below: After reaching a low of 26,000 in 1919, immigration through Ellis Island increased again to nearly 600,000 in 1921. Immigrants in the early 1920s went through a more intensive and time-consuming medical inspection and had to endure worsening conditions on the island. The attitude toward immigrants after World War I also grew increasingly hostile in the United States, leading to the enactment of severely restrictive immigration legislation in the 1920s.

Opposite, bottom: A group of German immigrants enjoys a midday meal in the Ellis Island dining area in 1926. Mealtime could be an adventure for newcomers, who often encountered new foods like bananas, ice cream, and sandwiches, and new ways of serving familiar foods.

Right: This kindergarten calisthenics class exemplifies the kinds of programs that Commissioner Howe attempted to bring to Ellis Island during his tenure from 1914 to 1919. Parents who found it difficult to wait around with restless children were no doubt relieved to have structured programs available for them.

Above: One of Frederic Howe's reform initiatives was to create classrooms for immigrant children in order to give them a productive way to pass the long hours on the island while their parents were being detained. Howe hired teachers who spoke a variety of languages.

Above: A small group of new arrivals disembarks in front of the main building in 1926. In contrast to the hordes during the peak immigration years, this crowd is minuscule. From 1892 through 1924, more than 14 million immigrants passed through Ellis Island, representing 71 percent of the total foreign-born population of the United States. From 1925 until its closing in 1954, Ellis Island saw only 2.3 million immigrants pass through. Yet this still represented more than half of all the newcomers entering the United States.

Above: A view of Ellis Island's main depot long after the peak years of immigration. Following World War I, prospective immigrants applied for visas at American consulates in their home countries and were given medical inspections there. After 1924, only those who had problems with their paperwork were detained at Ellis Island, along with war refugees and displaced persons.

CHAPTER SIX

The End of an Era

Under the harsh 1924 National Origins Act, prospective immigrants underwent inspection before they left their home countries, making the trip to Ellis Island less necessary. By 1932, America was in the grips of the Great Depression, and for the first time ever, more immigrants left the country than arrived. The climate in the United States was summed up well in the *Report of the Ellis Island Committee*, commissioned by the Department of Labor and published in 1934: "Against the illegal immigrant, we should proceed energetically. The country should employ every means to keep out the alien who is not entitled to admission. If he succeeds in crossing our borders, we should use every legal means to search him out and deport him promptly."

Despite these policies, immigrants continued to arrive in the United States, and many of them, including a new wave of European Jews, this time fleeing Nazism, came through Ellis Island. At the same time, however, the dismal U.S. economy also encouraged some Europeans to move back to their countries of origins in the belief that their work prospects might actually improve. By 1937, however, Ellis Island's population on any given day had been reduced to about 160 deportees and thirty immigrants awaiting detention, and throughout the remainder of that decade and the next, the island was primarily used as a detention center. As in the previous war, U.S. officials during World War II used Ellis Island to detain suspected U.S. enemies— Japanese, German, and Italian expatriates, as well as enemy merchant seamen. One thousand enemy aliens were under virtual house arrest on the island in 1943, and, later, under the Internal Security Act, suspected communists and fascists were rounded up and added to the detainee population.

By 1949, the U.S. Coast Guard had taken over much of the island for office and storage space. The final rationale for closing down the station was a 1954 Justice Department decree that gave detained aliens parole until a ruling board could hear their cases. In March 1955, the federal government declared Ellis Island surplus property and had it turned over to the General Services Administration.

For more than ten years, Ellis Island was virtually abandoned, and there were plans to sell the property. In 1965, however, a National Park Service proposal to make the site a national monument prevailed. In the largest project of its kind in U.S. history, the historic restoration of Ellis Island began in 1984 and was completed in September 1990, at a cost of $162 million. The "Island of Hope, Island of Tears" now stands as a monument to all who came through its doors.

Below: Immigrants cheer at the sight of the Statue of Liberty as they arrive at New York Harbor to embark on their new lives.

Above: Roughly nine out of one hundred immigrants were marked with an X for suspected mental deficiency and were sent to examination rooms for further testing. During this primary examination, doctors would begin by asking immigrants questions about themselves and then have them attempt to complete a puzzle, solve simple math problems, or count backward. In general, puzzle tests were favored to help determine any mental "defects," because they did not require translation. Here, a woman is tested by Dr. Howard Knox, the man who invented many of the puzzles and tests used to determine the mental fitness of immigrants passing through Ellis Island. Dr. Knox practiced medicine on the island from 1910 to 1916, where he perfected many of these diagnostic tools.

Above: A mother and child wait in an unusually quiet Registry Room. The emptiness of the hall suggests that this photo was taken during the later years of Ellis Island immigration or that this family was among the last to be inspected that day.

Above: Although millions of Jewish immigrants came to Ellis Island over its sixty-year history, this sukkah, the small hut used for meals during the Jewish holiday of Sukkoth, was the first of its kind ever built on the island. It was constructed by the Hebrew Immigrant Aid Society in the immigration station's final years.

Opposite: Over the years, the beautiful copper domes of Ellis Island's stately immigration station had deteriorated and threatened to collapse. Thanks to a major renovation, completed in 1990, the four cupola-topped towers can once again be appreciated by visitors. Today, the red-brick structure, with its ironwork and limestone trim, is one of the few remaining grand-scale brick buildings in New York.

Above: The relatively thin crowd of the post–peak immigration years. Nine hundred thousand immigrants were processed in 1914. By 1918, the numbers had dwindled to less than thirty thousand because of World War I and growing anti-immigrant sentiment. The rate increased again briefly after the war, but new restrictive laws led to a steadily declining immigrant flow beginning in 1925.

Sources

BOOKS

Brownstone, David M., Irene M. Franck, and Douglass Brownstone. *Island of Hope, Island of Tears.* New York: Metrobooks, 2002. (Reprint of Rawson, Wade Publishers 1979 edition.)

Burrows, Edwin G. and Mike Wallace. *Gotham: A History of New York City to 1898.* New York: Oxford University Press, 1999.

Coan, Peter Morton. *Ellis Island Interviews: In Their Own Words.* New York: Checkmark Books, 1998.

Glenn, Susan A. *Daughters of the Shtetl: Life and Labor in the Immigrant Generation.* Ithaca, NY: Cornell University Press, 1990.

Norton, Mary Beth, et al. *A People and a Nation: A History of the United States (Volume II: Since 1865).* New York: Houghton Mifflin, 2000. (Sixth edition.)

Palmer, Carleton H., *Report of the Ellis Island Committee, March 1934.* Englewood, NJ: Jerome S. Ozer, Publisher, 1971.

Reeves, Pamela. *Ellis Island: Gateway to the American Dream.* New York: Barnes & Noble Books, 2000.

Yans-McLaughlin, Virginia and Marjorie Lightman. *Ellis Island and the Peopling of America: The Official Guide.* New York: The New Press, 1997.

WEBSITES

American Park Network. *History: Ellis Island.*
www.americanparknetwork.com/parkinfo/sl/history/ellis.html

Brown Quarterly 4, no. 1 (Fall 2000).
http://brownvboard.org/brwnqurt/brwnqurt.htm

Ellis Island Immigration Museum, ARAMARK.
www.ellisisland.com

Hamill, Pete. The History Channel. historychannel.com/exhibits/ellisisle

Kraut, Alan M. *Records of the Immigration and Naturalization Service.* University Publications of America, 1995.
www.lexisnexis.com/academic/guides/immigration/ins/insa3.htm

National Park Service. *Ellis Island: Through America's Gateway.*
www.I-channel.com/education/ellis/

ThinkQuest. http://library.thinkquest.org/20619/Eihist.html

ORAL HISTORIES

The stories and quotes from individual immigrants were drawn from the following sources:

Jeanne Assidian, *Ellis Island Interviews: In Their Own Words* (Checkmark Books); Helen Barth, *Island of Hope, Island of Tears* (Viking Penguin); Marta Kazarian (pseudonym), American Immigration Museum, Oral History Project; Sophia Kreitzberg, Ellisisland.com; Georg Kruger (pseudonym), American Immigration Museum, Oral History Project; Harriet Kurzweil (pseudonym), American Immigration Museum, Oral History Project; Tony Sabatino (pseudonym), American Immigration Museum, Oral History Project.

Above: In a photograph from 1925, an immigrant family, their inspection complete, gazes toward the New York City skyline from the Ellis Island dock as they wait for the government ferry that will take them to Manhattan.

Photo Credits

Brown Brothers: pp. 6-7, 8-9, 12 bottom, 20-21, 24-25, 27, 30-31, 33, 35 top, 36-37, 40 bottom, 41, 42-43, 45, 46 top, 48 top, 52-53, 55, 59 top, 59 bottom, 60-61, 62, 65, 66 top, 66 bottom, 67 top, 70, 71, 74, 75 bottom, 76-77, 78 left, 78-79, 80-81, 81 right, 82 bottom, 85, 94, 95 top, 100 left, 100-101, 105, 106, 107 left, 107 right, 108-109, 114, 115 top, 116 left, 120 top, 120 bottom, 121, 124-125.

Corbis: 18, 58, 68 bottom, 87 top, 87 bottom, 98-99, 104, 105 top, 122, 126-127.

Museum of the City of New York: pp. 11 (gift of Joseph J. Nardone), 57, 95 bottom, 109 top, 109 bottom (The Leonard Hassam Bogart Collection).

National Archives: pp. 14-15, 16, 17, 19, 22-23, 28, 40 top, 46-47.

National Park Service Ellis Island National Monument: pp. 2-3, 10, 12 top, 22 left, 32, 34, 35 bottom, 38 bottom, 39, 44, 47 bottom, 48 bottom, 64 top, 64 bottom, 68 top, 69, 72, 86-87, 88-89, 91, 93, 94, 96, 97 bottom, 98 left, 110, 111, 118-119, 123; ©Alfred Stieglitz: p. 49.

New York Public Library: pp. 21 right, 47 top, 67 bottom, 75, 82-83; ©Lewis Hine: pp. 13, 43 right, 38 top, 50-51, 63, 73, 112 left, 112 right, 113, 115 bottom, 116-117.

State Historical Society of Wisconsin: pp. 84 top, 84 bottom, 102-103.

Index